Our Extraordinary Monsters

Our Extraordinary Monsters

Vanessa Moeller

Carolyn Marie Souaid, Editor

Signature Editions

Cover design by Doowah Design.
Cover artwork, "Glyph Sphere 122 TP1," by Peter Powning.
Photo of Vanessa Moeller by Mathieu Léger.

This book was printed on Ancient Forest Friendly paper.
Printed and bound in Canada by Marquis Book Printing Inc.

We acknowledge the support of The Canada Council for the Arts and the Manitoba Arts Council for our publishing program.

ACKNOWLEDGEMENTS
Ross Leckie, mentor, friend, editor — who saw a glimmer of promise in the initial debris — thank you. To those who helped my writing through various stages especially Brian Bartlett, Mark Jarman, Erin Moure, Anne Simpson, Karen Solie, Patricia Young, Sharon McCartney and Carolyn Marie Souaid with special thanks to Martin Middeke for his insights to help the translations become luminous. And to my vast array of family and friends who have helped me become the extraordinary monster I am — *Thank you, Danke Schön, Merci, Gracías...*

Library and Archives Canada Cataloguing in Publication

Moeller, Vanessa, 1977–
Our extraordinary monsters / Vanessa Moeller.

Poems.
ISBN 978-1-897109-35-9

I. Title.

PS8626.O433E98 2009 C811'.6 C2009-904906-6

Signature Editions
P.O. Box 206, RPO Corydon, Winnipeg, Manitoba, R3M 3S7
www.signature-editions.com

For my father, Alfred, my mother, Astrid, Marion & Andre
for being the pillars that held me upright my entire life;
Brittany, Zara & Nicholas who came later to let the light stream in.

And for Mathieu, the invisible watermark beneath some of the words,
who I found only after they had been written: Xo ∞+.

Contents

Sea Grounds Sky

Six Lost Butterflies

Shaping the Frame

Schlucke Deine Stiche

Signed Sincerely Yours

Currency of Moments

Sighting Invisible Cities

Notes on Poems

We are ourselves but we are also that extraordinary monster
made up of bits of someone else's longing, memories,
dreams, fears, needs, experiences and hopes.

—Alberto Manguel

Sea Grounds Sky

How do you say "to love" in the dialect of water?
In the language of earth, what part of speech are we?
—Yehuda Amichai

The Hydrography of Memory

You memorize the scar beneath my left collarbone while we wait
for the rain to end. Your fingers read its ridges like a sentence
in Braille where your thumbprint begins to delineate
interior chambers that echo a pattering resonance
of voices reciting childhood stories that unfurl in a pallor
as if released from nautilus shells: cracked clay jars spill
silver bullion, clouds of embalming oil, resin the colour
of mahogany. This sunken library of books still
unread, ebbs to the edge of my mind, flows away
when I attempt to grasp the moment when I was five, fell
asleep listening to my father's heartbeat, unaware that someday
its rhythm would cease and I'd have only a fragile eggshell
of memory's sounding. The drops thrum the window
as I turn from you, watch rain surrender to snow.

The Consciousness of Water

"We are more tears than bone," you said when I read
that our bodies are 70 per cent water. "Are you aware
that since we're more liquid than solid
we're attuned to minute frequencies? There
is a Japanese scientist named Emoto who
claims water is vulnerable to emotion. Exposed
to cold and music, distilled water is transcribed into
crystalline calligraphy, a fine molecular prose
whose fluency is texture not sound.
That's why when you are in a room
filled with a sonata a pulse seems to rise from the profound
recesses of your cells until soon
you are no longer rhythmed by your heart
but by something written two hundred years ago by Mozart."

The Keening of Icebergs

Geophysicists say it's like something from a horror
film — each iceberg weeps its own lament
when crevasses inside flow with water
and set its walls vibrating. But what is meant
by these keenings? This is the sound
of ice sundered — like oak bending
to break, like the tones of an abject viola found
in the calloused fingers that pluck a string
ready to snap, like a voice reduced to rasp
when words like *love* or *tomorrow* scrape
the throat, corrugate the tongue. To ask
what is meant is to wonder about the shape
of an hour, how to fit the body to its frame,
how a husk of prayer can encase a name.

The Afterlife of Pearls

Oysters transferred from water to land,
their soft labial folds pried open, forced
to accept fragments of metal, grains of sand
to create facsimiles whose luster is divorced
from the lost art of cliff diving, when men still knew
how to hold their breath between clenched
teeth as their bodies fell through air, plunged through
water's turquoise silence until lungs compressed
into an origami burn and hands groped, searching for
the skin of shells. How they cultivated
the unfolding patience of desire from the ocean's floor.
Now it is with deliberate touch that pearls are sculpted,
in vast beds no longer ocean-nurtured
but layered in nacreous greed and labeled cultured.

The Diaphony of Dunes

Friability. Stillness. The barest shift
to the deliquescence of adamantine
grains, sudden damascene patterns drift
down the sides of dunes, each design
an aleatoric hum. The operatic bravura
begins an avalanche where each carom
is heavy with natural coloratura.
The scientific art of composing music from
layers of sand, each song an attrition
until physicists admit after thirty days
the dunes are left mute, the friction
at the crystalline edges frays
and leaves songs tattered,
the desert lyrics irrevocably blurred.

The Pulse of Trees

Bare branches stretched like veins across the blue
wrist of the sky. Trees as evidence
that the earth has a heart. Wooden arteries breaking through
the ground remind us of the presence
of a burning core that keeps us alive, moving through the mist
of years, decades, through the elliptical curve of orbit.
Your own heart, small as a clenched fist,
seems to weigh next to nothing but is there, its fit
perfect in the bare bone cage of your
ribs. Untangle its knot of vessels, stretch the empty
threads into a bleeding equator,
and circle the world two and a half times. The mystery
at our centre a milky area in the human heart with no function,
that some claim is the soul's physical manifestation.

The Vibrato of Volcanoes

A seismic thumb pressed to the edge of plate
until the tectonic trembles into a wavered note
that tides out where the viscous margins vibrate
    shift under the corals of oceans, beneath remote
expanses of savannah. In most places a chord so
bated it cannot be heard, only sensed in the fins
of goldfish, carried clear in the moon jelly's flow,
transcribed by the patterned ins
and outs of a fine needle skimming wide spools
of paper. But in others, craters narrow
to gather the movement where energy pools,
tephra and lava escape the marrow
of the earth, rise until the quaver can be felt in
the foot's arch, the pelvis's hollow, the heart's skin.

The Psalms of Clouds

The halo of cirrostratus artists placed
around the heads of saints who suffered and died
for their miracles, the paint shaping each face
that saw the history of heaven written in the sky
into some variation of pain or veneration.
Cirrus uncinus, feathers detached from the wings
of angels who crash to earth after rejecting the degeneration
of paradise, who learn to live under our altostratus ceilings,
walk the streets with charred nubs that protrude
hideously from shoulder blades they hide under
old coats and dirty sweaters. Today those who exude
any divine shadow, any remaining smudge of wonder
are broken by the symmetry of altocumulus.
Such simple miracles no longer convince the rest of us.

The Archeology of Air

Air as artifact that could reveal history's layers of connection —
how it's filtered through the interior matrices of leaves.
How it's cupped in creased hands in foreign
countries, carried to the mouth and molded to reprieves
or words of blessing. Exhaled over two hundred years ago in
the moan of a woman in the throes of a nightmare,
her hands drenched in gold dust, her panic like the thin
high note of a piano hit hard, once, in a silent room. This air
embroidered with a fugue of violins before it drifted out to sea
inhaled by a swimming girl. How we remain unaware
of lives hidden beneath the debris,
forgotten, dusted with time and threadbare,
waiting to be discovered and told but these stories
will remain hidden until we learn how to excavate a breeze.

The Mythology of Winds

He lay beside her as she was falling asleep and told
her of winds: "The Boreas is an unexpected kiss where
a thin sliver of ice is passed between lips, melts over the threshold.
A small gust of the Levanto is the hot despair
of a fevered child exhaled against your
throat, pooling in the hollow where your collarbones
descend and fuse, catch shadow and contour.
The Etesian is a stolen length of cool silk in tones
of grey laid over the long planes of a naked body
that is warm, unexpecting. The Sumatra is a feather traced
over the length of your palm, over the filigree
of lines that allows you to feel the delicate net of nerves laced
below the glistening waves of skin."
Finally, he closed his arms around her, harboured her inhalation.

Six Lost Butterflies

There are nine different words in Maya for the color blue but just three Spanish translations, leaving six butterflies that can be seen only by the Maya, proving beyond a doubt that when a language dies, six butterflies disappear from the consciousness of the earth.

— Earl Shorris

Drenched Prose

"The rain is my favourite thing in the world besides sex..." — S.F.

It is best when it begins haltingly, with tentative touch, anticipatory as rhythm rises. It can make the room evolve, feel capacious and possible. You have to find ways to inhabit this space, shape your body into nooks and expanses, allow the Morse code of your pulse to align with its cadences. It leaves the air either muzzy, your breath a cobwebbed sigh, or tears it open, reminds you that *vitality* is a word with edges. It can string your body into tensile expectancy for something elemental, the petrichor rising from the depth of loam, from the inside of thigh. Or it calms you until you settle like silt. And you spread yourself into it, gather moisture into your pores, wait, writhe with impatience, sink, calm, rise again, come.

Awaited Reply

After a letter from Katia Grubisic

A decade later, as a woman,
I stood on Langestraße
and tipped back my umbrella
to reassure myself of the truth of rain
on my eyelids.
I wrapped the sensation around myself
as one would a coat that bears
the cologne of someone passed.
I sheltered under the canopy
of a street vendor, chose a pomegranate
and held it to my lips, inhaled,
vermilion staining my tongue.
Words saccharine, gritty,
clotted my mouth and left me
unable to explain to the man arranging pears
"I want this one" or "I wish the rain would end."

This city is not my home but my mother's.
It bears down with brick and traffic,
and it contains half my language
halb meiner Sprache, halb meiner Stimme.
The other half arrives in creased envelopes
with your handwriting that stretches
a thousand miles of distance taut,
your words explaining
how, at the All-You-Can-Eat Breakfast Buffet,
you wrote me this letter on the back of a placemat,
its left corner greased from stray scrambled egg,
a stain I can't help touch as I read the line:
I saw wild horses and thought of you.

Perfumed Sentence

...a perfume is not the same as a sentence...
—David Howes

Don't tell me that perfume
cannot be a sentence,
that trees are not language,
because to deny this
is to deny that hands
can be cathedrals,
which was proven by Rodin,
bronze fingertips timbered
to create a room
walled by palms.

I know that
perfume is a sentence
because the rounded vowels
of labdanum
entwine with the consonants
of oakmoss
until heart notes fade into
base notes
that press into the Cambrian rock
of memory.

Scent lingers but cannot
be contained
by porous sheets of skin
stretched over a spire
of metacarpals,
faint but fossilized
in a pattern of neurons.
I know that perfume is a sentence
because it is how I remember you –
with the articulate longhand of musk.

Evanescent List

I am learning the list of what I do not own.
—Karen Connelly

I do not own the creak of crickets
like a hundred rusted keys
turning in locks again and again
or the frictive, smoke-drenched timbre
of your voice telling stories of alchemists making
clocks from the wings of owls.
I cannot confine marizipan's cloying melt,
nor can I take the sweet
hay taste dehiscing into July's air
away from home. I have no engram
to contain the emollient stroke
of my grandmother's hand and no way
to dulcify the excoriating touch
of my abusive ex-lover.
I cannot bottle the cologne
my grandfather wore since I can barely
keep my own perfume from lassitude.
I do not possess the glaze of scent
that rises from a horse's mane,
or the smell of moss decaying
in the gamboge light of autumn.
And I will never own the reflection
of my reflection
in my own eye in the mirror
or the thousand matryoshka copies
of myself held therein.

Linguistic Obituary

> *It is not merely a writer's conceit to think that the human world is made of words and to remember that no two words in all the world's languages are alike. Of all the arts and sciences made by man, none equals a language, for only a language in its living entirety can describe a unique and irreplaceable world.*
>
> —*Earl Shorris*

For this eulogy I write dictionaries to fill the lacunae
where words gathered meaning
like empty gourds collect rainwater.
A word in Kaskean expressed
the texture of butterfly wings pressed between lips;
another discerned the smell of a woman
still slick with sex, described as feral,
woodsy, slightly metallic.

In Palaic, names for
the crease where a horse's ear meets neck,
the soreness of a pressed bruise,
the tang of an old person's bedridden body,
and two words that, when placed together,
gestured toward the moment of realization
when foot's arch encounters sharp beach rock.

How the Kalapuya people could speak of the sound
of apiaries on fire, of the ululation of nocturnal
predators searching for lost young. Now there is
no chocolate-melt to describe the colour of the ocean
in the February of Mahican. No saccharine tones of Dororo
left to tell how regret
erodes the back of the eyes until you no longer see
the world, or yourself, in the same way.

Shaping the Frame

For my mother

We started out alone with our mothers, in the womb,
and we got to know them from the inside, internally.
We grew our bones and our hearts inside our mothers.
—*Lorna Crozier*

Shaping the Frame

For my imagined daughter

To give birth to a small husk of storied molecules,
my father's hands, my mother's eyes, my angle of jaw
and a curve of lip from a great-great-great ancestor
whose identity is just beyond the long branches
of the family tree fading in the sitting room.

When my body begins to erode, age scuffing away
my surfaces, you will begin to fully inhabit
the chamber of your name, learn to siphon
knowledge from the world and rearrange it
to fit the nooks and alcoves of your character.

Eventually I will be disincarnated, reduced to
flecks and wind, but you will read me again
in the syntax of your own daughter's body,
quixotic sylph who grows into the length
of a spine that reminds you of teak.

Den Rahmen bilden

Für meine eingebildete Tochter

Eine kleine Schale von geschichteten Molekülen zu gebären:
meines Vaters Hände, meiner Mutter Augen, meines Kiefers Winkel
und die Windung der Lippe eines ur-ur-ur Verwandten
dessen Identität hinter den langen Zweigen
des im Zimmer verwelkt liegenden Stammbaums steckt.

Wenn mein Körper anfängt zu erodieren, die Reife
meiner Oberflächen abkratzt, wirst Du anfangen die Kammer
Deines Namens ganz zu bewohnen, wirst lernen, wie man der Welt
Erfahrung absaugt und die dann umordnet,
um sie den Ecken und Nischen Deines Karakters anzupassen.

Endlich werde ich disinkarniert, in Teilchen und Wind
vermindert, aber Du wirst mich wieder lesen
in dem Satzbau deines Kindes,
in dieser phatastichen Sylphe, die in die Länge ihrer Wirbelsäule
wächst bis sie Dich an einen Teakholzbaum errinert.

Growing the Voice

My mother's voice is nothing like my own
which is wind and wet moss,
where my vowels sometimes reveal
my body's equine suppleness
my spine is a sentence that reads:
I was never tall enough to write on the sky.

The idea for paper grew from the bodies of wasps
while the idea for my life was written
in a double-helixed script, a correspondence
between bodies that led to my birth
into the spaciousness of my mother's voice,
its honey-written-on-vellum cadences.

Now I walk through the world with mirrors for eyes.
Carry a language of warmed amber in my mouth.

Die Stimme entwickeln

Die Stimme meiner Mutter ist überhaupt nicht wie meine,
die wie Wind und nasses Moos ist,
in der meine Vokale manchmal
die pferdehafte Biegsamkeit meines Körpers preisgeben;
meine Wirbelsäule ist ein Satz der lautet:
Ich war nie groß genug um auf den Himmel zu schreiben.

Die Idee des Papiers erwuchs aus Wespenkörpern,
die Idee meines Lebens wurde verfasst in einer
Doppelhelix-Schrift, eine Korrespondenz
zwischen Körpern, die zu meiner Geburt
in die Geräumigkeit meiner Mutter Stimme und
deren Honig-auf-Pergament-geschriebene Kadenzen führte.

Nun wandere ich durch die Welt mit Spiegeln als Augen.
Trage eine Sprache erwärmten Bernsteins in meinem Mund.

Untying the Breath

When I was six I learned
to unbraid my vocal chords,
weave them into an angular
pattern of English instead of the
familiar orbed syntax of German
that had sheltered me since birth.

My mouth hollowed by the absence
of words like *sanft* and *Mitternacht*,
left unable to explain *Leidenschaft*,
since no translation fuses
suffering and creation into a single word
meant to express passion.

Eventually I learned to untangle
the Gordian threads of breath and accent
until my voice became cobwebbed
enough to sift away the vaporous
and leave only the gracile syllables
and the definition of a loess.

Den Atem entfesseln

Als ich sechs war lernte ich,
meine Stimmbänder zu entflechten,
um sie in das kantige Muster
des Englischen zu weben statt in
die gewohnte Syntax des Deutschen,
die mir seit der Geburt Schutz bot.

Ausgehölt war mein Mund von der Abwesenheit
von Wörtern wie *sanft* und *Mitternacht*;
war unfähig *Leidenschaft* zu erklären,
denn keine Übersetzung kann Leiden und Schaffen
in ein einziges Wort verschmelzen um
damit Passion auszudrücken.

Irgendwann einmal lernte ich doch
den gordischen Knoten von Atem und Akzent
zu lösen bis meine Stimme ein solch dichtes Spinnennetz
wurde um Dämpfe noch zu sieben und
nur grazile Silben übrig zu lassen und
die Definition von Löß.

Molding the Tongue

I learned
to grasp
the language,
to mold
words that
were metallic
and thin
as thimbles,
sculpt sentences
so they
rested like
long rivers
down the
length of
my tongue,
weighed it
down like
silver coins
placed there
to make
crossing possible.

Die Zunge ausformen

Ich lernte
die Sprache
zu greifen,
Worte zu formen,
metallisch
und dünn
wie Fingerhüte,
Sätze so zu bilden,
dass sie wie
lange Flüsse
die ganze Strecke
meiner Zunge
hinunter liefen,
und sie beschwerten
wie Silbermünzen,
die dort
hingelegt wurden,
um einen Übergang
möglich zu machen.

Binding the Wings

How, when I understood mortality,
time became smooth black beach stones
I carried in my pockets while I read
hagiographies, corseted in the narrative
of lives where convictions
lixiviated any trace of disbelief
from corporeal forms.

I no longer fear death for I have faith
that someday my body
will dissolve, my arms will reveal
they were never flesh,
but a thick-fisted bundle of moths
that will loosen
                                        and release to the air.

Die Flügel binden

Wie sehr die Zeit, als ich Sterblichkeit verstand,
zu glatten schwarzen Strandkieseln wurde,
die ich in meinen Taschen trug
während ich Hagiographien las und
verschnürt war in Schilderungen von Leben,
in denen Überzeugungen Körpern
jede Spur des Zweifelns entzogen.

Ich fürchte mich nicht länger vor dem Tod,
denn ich vertraue darauf, dass sich mein Körper
eines Tages auflöst, dass meine Arme
offenbaren, dass sie niemals Fleisch waren,
sondern ein dichtes Bündel Motten,
die sich losreißen
                    und in die Luft entfliehen.

Schlucke Deine Stiche

For my father

In Turkish, the word muhabbet means both "conversation" and "love."
You say for both, "To do muhabbet."
I like the idea of conversation being a window into one's heart or mind.
—Alberto Manguel

15.02.68

Habe mich mit meiner Maschine
auf die Terrasse begeben,
um zu versuchen, Dir einen Brief
zu schreiben, ich schreibe versuchen,
weil ich damit erschränkend sagen möchte,
daß ich nicht weiß, ob ich noch heute damit fertig werde,
denn ich möchte Dir soviel sagen,
über meine Gedanken schreiben,
denn da ich ja körperlich kaum beschäftigt bin,
habe ich dadurch so sehr viel Zeit,
Gedanken zu bewegen,
und ich möchte Dich daran teilnehmen lassen.

02.15.06

Lorca professed to wanting
only a hand, a broken hand if possible.
I look at mine, carbon copies
of yours and as I type this,
I realize my fingers are the perfect size
to fit these keys. The first knuckles
of all your fingers were broken at different times
(a horse kick, a mis-swung
hammer, a jammed gear), how you
couldn't be bothered
to get them reset so they healed
into 45 degree angles.
Those overly large hands
my mother complained about,
remembering the days
when you were manicured,
wore tailored suits,
smelled of Aramis cologne.

I loved your broken hands,
the meaty fingers,
the rasp of palm's callus.

20.03.68

Gestern war nun mein 29. Geburtstag –
ein nicht gerade berauschendes Ereignis.

Das bedeutet, daß ich alt geworden bin –
besser älter, obschon ich mich nur wenig älter fühle,
lediglich reifer.

Auch das Resümmé, was ich dann ziehen müßte,
war nicht gerade überwältigend,
denn bisher sind meine Leistungen ja noch mehr als dünn.

Es wird also Zeit, etwas zu schaffen.

Leichter gesagt als getan.

05.08.06

My 29th birthday.

An age where my memories
are amassing at such speed
I'm unsure where to place them
in my personal chronology, how to
bear those with a mass that keeps
the arches of my feet slightly bowed
down towards the earth:

That spring morning. A breeze that was cold cashmere
and warm mint. I overheard you say I'd start school
in the fall — my momentary vertigo,
where the size of the world, all my possible futures,
pressed against my five-year-old body.

                    I, too, continue to ripen,
          am resuming the art of
weaving the chords
of my voice into
                    something
easier said than done.

You smelled of creosote and straw that September afternoon.
I embraced you and you finally admitted:
I don't know what's wrong. I seem to just keep losing words.

22.03.68

Es wird Dir auffallen,
wie häufig ich
von solchem Künstlerschaffen schreibe,
ich möchte gern schriftstellerisch
etwas zustande bringen,
habe auch oft,
wenn ich in der Sonne träume
oder vor dem Einschlafen,
Gedanken, die ich sehr klar
in Sätze bringen kann
einschließlich der Interpunktion,
als wäre ich bereits beim Schreiben,
und die es auch wert wären eingedruckt
der Nachwelt überliefert zu werden,
obwohl sich dies vielleicht aus meinem Mund
sehr überheblich anhört.

05.28.06

I once asked you
why you never wrote
when you came to this country.

I don't know which language to write in, you admitted.

When you came here,
you still dreamed in German
but slowly English seeped in
and left you adrift

I'm somewhere in between, you tried to explain.

I(ch) understand/verstehe es now.

Write in both, flechte sie zusammen.

03.04.68

Oft möchte ich Anlauf nehmen
und diese Gedanken auf Papier bringen,
aber sobald ich so real denke über diese Dinge,
schon die Wahl ob Maschine
                                oder Handschrift
bereitet Schwierigkeiten,
ist mir als wären diese Gedanken
durch mein Gehirn
                wie durch ein Sieb
                                        auf und davon,
ich weiß nicht,
ob sie dann der Ansicht sind,
sie wären es nicht wert,
zu Papier gebracht zu werden.

03.04.06

There were other languages
you were already writing:

You took
          367 acres of land
and turned them articulate,
                    fields,
a green calligraphy,
          the sinewed prose
                              in the muscle clench of
the horses you helped raise,
                                        the stream
you rewrote into a lake
and the decrepit
                              farmhouse you composed
          into *home.*

15.04.68

Ich habe mich hier vielleicht
etwas schwulstig ausgedrückt,
aber das liegt daran, daß in mir der Schriftsteller –
falls überhaupt einer schlummert –
noch nicht erwacht ist,
obwohl für mich diese Sätze
so klar sind wie die Augen der Kinder.

Vielleicht werden sie aber auch Dir klar sein,
was mich dann würde hoffen lassen,
daß ich doch wenigstens für einen Menschen,
der zwar den anderen gegenüber sehr im Vorteil ist,
da er mit mir auf einer gedanklichen Wellenlänge geschaltet ist,
klar würde schreiben können.

03.08.06

I don't know how to reply
to this version of you.
It requires a choreography
of the mouth
that leaves me motionless. Speechless.

I want my words to
                    twist through
              yours
         like a vanilla trumpet vine
our meanings interlaced
   until sepal protects petal.

04.05.68

Oft ertappe ich mich dabei,
über Dich, für Dich Gedichte zu beginnen,
ein Ding was vielleicht nie Papier erreichen wird,
was aber mir wiederum zeigt,
was alles in mir vorhanden ist,
was ich sonst bestimmt als nicht existierend bezeichnet hätte.
Ist das ein Zeichen von Verrücktheit
oder Überspanntheit?
Ich weiß es nicht.

03.02.06

Even when your mind could
no longer find the tendrils that
connected words to the world,
you never lost the filament
binding me to the pet name you gave.
When they asked, *Who is that?*
I was left to explain, *That's right. That's his nickname for me.*

I don't know why

                    you remembered it, were able to keep it tethered.
Was I the poem you wanted to write,
an eloquence that could only be expressed
          as *daughter?*

25.05.68

Es ist wunderbar einsam dort —
nur große schwarze Krabben und die Gischt
der Brandung. Meine Schriftstellerei
wird mir selbst bald zur Force,
denn ich bin nur dann in der Lage zu schreiben.
Dann kommen die Worte, die Gedanken
und ich schreibe viele verschiedene Versionen
über verschiedene Themen.

Bin ich wieder im Dorf, zerreiße ich alles Geschriebene,
weil ich nicht daran glaube.
Sind das Minderwertigkeitskomplexe?
Oder bin ich doch schriftstellerisch
unfruchtbar?
Ich bin nicht sicher und werde weiter versuchen,
etwas Gescheites fertigzubringen.

02.24.06

The body simplified —
          gauzy layers of onion-skin
meticulously peeled away
          to reveal a blooming
anemone in your left temporal lobe.

I became the only one
who could translate you,
                    somehow able to
puzzle out the gesture of your eyes,
the cadences of your breathing,
into sentences
                    of need or want.

Those last days
          as your body became a thinning sentence
     I became
          your lexicon.
                    I gave you meaning.

26.06.68

Mein Buch
ist noch nicht
weiter gediehen —
zur Zeit
ist nichts drin.

Aber ich will die Hoffnung
nicht aufgeben,
daß doch eines Tages
hier noch der Knoten reißt.

07.07.06

Your book
was written
in the vernacular
of pine tree,
and wood smoke.
Every morning
a new page
of dew or frost
punctuated by your boots
walking to the barn.

02.07.68

Sag mir was Du denkst,
Du brauchst mich nicht zu schonen,
denn nichts ist gefährlicher
als in Luftschlössern allein zu leben,

man muß auch gelengtlich
          wieder auf die Erde —

so schön wie das erstere wäre.

04.17.06

I try to keep the memory of you
in archival quality, aware of the danger
that too much exposure will erode it.
Instead I hide it behind
                                        the parclose of my sternum
                                              in the fluting of my clavicle
          protected
                                             but still light enough to carry.

07.07.68

Ich fühle Deine Zeilen alle,

schlucke Deine Stiche.

08.10.06

I
unfold my grief like a creased silk scarf.

Your memory is the only talisman I carry with me on this journey.

Mein Herz ist ein offener Gedankenmarkt.

Performance of *Schlucke Deine Stiche*

Schlucke Deine Stiche is a polyphonic score for two interpenetrating voices. The text of the poems is meant to be read out loud simultaneously so the voices speak to each other, overlap, interweave and echo across languages and temporal spaces. The German text is taken from letters written by my father in 1968 at the age of 29 while living in the Canary Islands for six months. The English text is my response across this 37-year gap, answering as his daughter at the same age, grappling with some of the same issues and ideas that he articulates. *Schlucke Deine Stiche* becomes a bilingual, cross-generational, bicultural and bi-worldly poetic dialogue across the silent space of 37 years where the voice of the woman I am in 2006 mingles and replies to the voice of the man who would become my father.

English translations of the German poems in *Schlucke Deine Stiche* are in the Notes on Poems section (page 103).

Signed Sincerely Yours

Every day we subtly revise who we think we are.
— Diane Ackerman

Postcard of El Teide, Black and White

Arrival felt like dressing
in honey,
my body sheathed
in ochre light
all accentuated nakedness
beneath.
Where do I begin?
How do I explain
the sound of squid
whipped on the rocks
outside my window?

They have no bones
to break, no clean snapped
entry into death
but something embogged —
a defeat marked
by tentacled stillness,
by the abandoned grasp
for stones
or any anchorage.

This diminuendo into afternoon
is almost worse.
I want to sign this *sincerely*.

Postcard of Dog Seated in Front of Banana Field

The man's fingers
have been climbing
an arpeggio staircase
of steel string
all evening,
the edge of tones
tinted cinnamon
before they evaporate.
Flamenco.
Sueños de una Guitarra.

Sueños. Dreams.

I think of home, the four hours and ocean that separate us.
Of you folding yourself into the narrative of a book,
your large hands rougher than the pages
and still scented with horseflesh and hay,
surrounded by a dull hum of summer.
I wonder what details I'll miss while I'm here —
the fine gravel, three withered daisy petals,
the smudge of pollen you'll find
rolled in the cuff of your jeans tonight.

Postcard of Local Proudly Displaying Shark Jaw

Old women haggle over
the price of papaya,
over whether weight denotes worth.
Hand gestures. *Cuarenta pesetas.*
Exchange. *Nada más.*
I walk past stands, my sneakers'
slow squeak cuts through the lulling hum
of fruit flies. Torpid strawberries
glow in overripe inertia,
their sick sweetness undercut
by a tint of gouda
or cured meats, ocean.

Sardines, Turkish wrasse, emperor fish, angel shark
symmetrical rows of glossy bodies,
round milky eyes still shocked,
not completely mute.
I run my finger along the cool silvered
curve of a swordfish and wonder
if this is why we close the eyes
of our dead, weigh them shut
with coins, afraid we might read
some last sight in the retina.
The vendor leans down with a gaping smile,
Solamente dos mil pesetas, señorita.

Postcard of Initials Carved into Dragon Tree

Saffron under my fingernails,
nostrils singed by the red peppers
from the back garden wall
as I concentrate on the geometric tempo
of blade through onion, the tiny
glassy panes that peel my eyes.

Aunt Helga said everyone should know how to
cook, how to take pieces of the world
and make them nourishing.

She is outside, engrossed in the measured
art of bread. Soon I expect the rooms
will be blanketed in a warm yeastiness.

Steam rises. There is a transformation
from form to malleability
of the perciatelli noodles
that reminds me of my own vertebrae's
domino collapse onto chairs, into beds.

The family eats dinner outside at a stone table
with volcanic mountains to our left
and the ocean to our right.
I am beginning to understand
what *satiated* means.

I am learning to answer my own hunger.

Postcard of Girl Intently Listening to Found Seashell

Translucent yellow bleeds to tangerine.
These flowers offer new problems
of translation. *Brugmansia sanguinea,*
also known as Angel Trumpets.

According to the plant guide:
They are perfect for a party
in the moonlight. But beware
of their dark side. Every part
of this plant is poisonous
if ingested.

Whelmed by heat I imagine such a party –
the peau-de-soie cool of night, a waft
of disembodied voices, the winnow
of ombre petals gesturing like luring fingers:
Come close, come closer. Taste me.

And who could resist the temptation
to crush such beauty between their teeth,
to swallow sanguinity, darkness
and the toxic possibility of angels?

Postcard of Child Dwarfed Next to Agave

A pentatonic scale of metatarsals,
slight glissando shifts as I carve
ocean with board fins, etch curves across
fluid viridian rising above me, over me,
down. It is an art that requires
balance trellised through nerves,
of knowing when to take a breath,
when to brace for the subaqueous sostenuto
of lung-burned panic, how to surrender
the immersed body to current,
peer through the Gaussian blur of water
to sky, surface into
a clear narration of sunlight.

On the beach, mouth against forearm,
the taste of my own body —
wax, oiled coconut, salt, not mine but
briny, that stings my chapped lips,
a husk
visible only to the tongue.

Postcard of Tattooed Glyphs Running Down Spine

I am burnished.
My body arcs
from day
deep into wave's gravity
and threads back up —
a surfacing whereupon
I wonder
how to live
here
above the ocean's
skin while my own
is eroded
by tides and salt.

How difficult
this attempt to keep
the world outside
when seawater
is carried so easily
in the eye,
when its taste
is a reminder of cuts
nursed by a tongue.

Constant osmosis,
a need for equilibrium
that does not allow
for any clear
delineation —
my eyelids
too thin
to block
the sunlight.

Postcard of Tide Reaching El Médano

Morning reaches me first with
sound: distanced murmurs of tourists
who amble boardwalks, talk about home,
the expense of meals, how
so-and-so really shouldn't sunbathe in the nude.
Undertones of waves, dog barks, ship creaks,
a rustling of banana leaves.
Then the smell of the warm croissants
freshly delivered and hanging from the front door,
a musky updraft of ripening fruit
and dying flowers, a hint of ocean,
brewing Moroccan coffee.
A calefacient lick of sunbeams
on my exposed soles, a tickle of breeze
over my bare shoulders, exposed nape
as I taste last night's dinner of calamari tapas
and wine not quite erased by toothpaste.

I don't need to open my eyes
to know you are gone,
the only clue of your presence
during the night is the grit of sand
pasted to my moist left wrist,
your scent woven
into the cotton fiber of the pillows,
entwined with my tousled hair.

Postcard of Avenida Jardines del Duque

That night the gecko became a half-moon scar
asleep against the white ceiling. The balcony door was open
even though the rain tapered from the sky, the thick green leaves
suddenly the skin of drums, heavy with rhythm.
The air lifted the fly-netting from my back
as I dreamt of dissolving into this earth,
my hair transformed into curling trellises
that flower into brilliant panicles of bloom.
I placed my mouth against the interior skin of forearm
and could still taste the ocean, the same ocean I fought
all summer who, like a deranged lover, had washed me up
against the volcanic cliffs until my legs were etched
with wounds, permanent petroglyphs of this journey.
I finally gave up trying to write descriptions in letters,
instead allowed lizards to crawl across the paper,
transcribe the script onto their pale bellies
and carry it into the shade of the orange flame vine
beneath the Chinese cracker flower. Words became impotent in the heat
and I grew to understand the cool understated prose of silence.
That last night each moment was an opening
of pores, of tiny doorways; a sensuous translation
into a language in which I would never truly be fluent.

Postcard of Hand Holding Three Fish Hooks

Your copy of *The Cinnamon Peeler*
and tucked between page 142
and 143, a photograph.
Her, framed in a greasy mirror,
the background an aperture
of ferns and a sky so bright
she is a blurred grisaille.
On the back you'd written a note in pencil:
fruit from the cork tree emits a smell
like turpentine when it is bruised.

I imagine a pervious bamboo door opening out into
a plash of Golden Rain trees whose seeds
you fashioned into necklaces, bracelets
that slipped from her thin wrists
when she ran from you, left
the path for a skein of African tulip trees
whose red tubular fingers lifted strands
of her hair, a caress she barely noticed
while an unnecessary jealousy uncoiled
within you. She stood just beyond reach, the body
of a black cat mink-slick in her arms
as she walked around the small dirt yard
and named each plant for you:
Elephant Ear Acacia, Flame of the Forest, Camel Thorn.
Your own unexpected Eve, barefoot and dusty.
How you suspected she was lying,
making up names as she went,
but you took the picture anyway —
any way to keep her.
And you returned, alone,
to spend the night
memorizing the joints of bamboo,
unable to keep the light contained.

I've pulled the fly-netting back, have abandoned writing
the navy sheets into the insomniac twists
of my body. I think about where you might be now,
what she may be doing at this moment as I exist
in the room's absinthe glow.

Porous walls allow the jungle in.
Staring at the scabrous ceiling I want to
jump on the bed, laugh, white flecks of paint descending
all around me,
remember winter,
sign this *love*.

Currency of Moments

Everything is biographical... What we make, why it is made, how we draw a dog, who it is we are drawn to, why we cannot forget. Everything is collage, even genetics. There is the hidden presence of others in us, even those we have known briefly. We contain them for the rest of our lives, at every border that we cross.

—Michael Ondaatje

I.

Postcard of Small Girl Eating Large Cotton Candy in Front of Ferris Wheel at Night

8 hours, 43 minutes and 17 seconds of flight.
Sat next to a woman who imports the dead into family photographs.
Loved ones provide a photo of the deceased; she arranges the living
so there is space to add ghosts later.
The beauty of the digital age, she declared.
I looked at the work and thought,
Everyone is sad except the dead who don't realize
they're already gone.

Now, I am here.

How do I spend this currency of moments?

II.

Postcard of Broken Scissors Half Buried in Desert Sand

It's the intimacy I miss, the oubliettes of the body,
being pressed against you:
the shell-tide echo next to my ear,
clench of heartbeat, blood pause,
long threads of air snaking through lung,
wet slosh of organs creating energy,
the imagined sound of cells as they die
or rebuild
or branch into some future death.

And I remember the afternoon you declared,
When I'm with you I feel like my heart's trapped in amber.
I remained silent but thought,
Mine is preserved in formaldehyde.

I don't believe in signing anything *with love*.

III.

Postcard of Torreros Watching Bullfight from Behind Protective Wall

Today I learned *araña* is Spanish for spider
    and chandelier.
So I wonder how to explain the *araña* that is spinning a web
in the *araña* above my head.
                                        Translations are always past imperfect.

IV.

Postcard of Cracked Carnival Mask at the Bottom of a Flight of Stairs

The souvenirs I'll take with me:

From the alchemist's shop:
A vial filled with lashes cried from the eyes of virgins.
A pamphlet entitled *Spiegelwelt* with all text written on pages of mirror
so if you glance beyond the words you have to face yourself.
A comb made of braided hair and fish bone.
An urn of Siberian rainwater collected during an eclipse.

From my walks:
Sound of chimes in the monsoon.
Cinnamon that still clings to the cuffs of my white shirt.
The title of a book I saw: *How To Grow Tall Enough To Write On The Sky.*

From you:
One letter, its edges smudged with fingerprints
still carrying a hint of oregano, tomato
enough I can imagine you at the stove
stealing a taste with a dip of finger
before returning to the page to write:
It is evening. Every day I watch the weather channel
so I know how your days will be.

I leave with nothing but a suitcase of elegies.

V.

Postcard of Ancient Forest Filled with Stilt Walkers Playing Hide and Seek

10 hours, 4 minutes and a handful of seconds
before I attempt re-entry into the confines of my old life.

Now when I look in mirrors I am reminded
of your collage of a woman's face
where you used only my eyes clipped from an old photo.
Disconcerting to have your history gaze back at you
from the face of a stranger.

Soon, I will depart and although my features
remain unaltered, someone else gazes
back from within that familiar mask.

I am completely spent.

Yours, with love,

Sighting Invisible Cities

Memory's images, once they are fixed in words, are erased...
— Italo Calvino

Archivist's Note:
Collection consists of ten letters written in an unidentified hand found in box in a burnt-out mask-making shop named La Moretta. *Items presumably scarred by the same fire that decimated the shop, the letters have no clear destination or addressee and seem to have been sent from destinations unknown, from within the borders of invisible cities. Located in Special Collections. Text in English. Access restricted.*

Letter from Adelma

Archivist's Note: MsC 073-01. Written on tissue paper in black ink. Writing characteristics suggest female (evaluated by handwriting specialist – see supplementary endnotes). Minimal water damage in addition to fire damage. Due to condition, manuscript too delicate to handle by hand.

Dear

arrived safely in A

cemetery met a widow whose arms were filled with red fleshy blossoms. She explained how she planted these flowers (which she claimed are named *Remembered Histories*) where she believed her husband's heart was located, the roots descending, nourished by his collapsing arteries. She cut the stems in bloom and placed one on his vacant pillow at night, pretended it was his scent. ~~Can you remember this way?~~ She offered me one and it seemed too intimate to take and rude to refuse. My hands smell of it still – it is the scent of vanilla if vanilla were crimson colored. Perhaps this paper still carries some trace. Can you sense it? Even across our distance?

Then

every face in the crowd a mask photocopied — how do we come to that point in our lives when every person met reminds us of someone else — not déja-vu ~~but~~ more like traveling a Möbius strip until

I can't explain how s

and the rain is incessant now

Letter from Argia

Archivist's Note:
MsC 073-02. Written on thick hotel issue stationery (trace evidence of hotel letterhead burned away from top right hand corner of page). Handwriting is very neat, ink used is Prussian blue, presumably from a fountain pen.

It is almost too ~~quiet~~ still. I feel a little stir crazy inhabiting the sterile confines of the hotel room (number 1026, easy to remember because of that anniversary). I'm always ~~surprised~~ startled by how so many people can inhabit such a close space, our dense honeycomb of rooms, and never have any real contact. We slide by each other like specters without ever really passing through anyone.

the sheets are a little damp, smell of bleach and

finally I pressed my ear to the floor of my room, expecting, perhaps, some faint echo from below, some equivalent to the ocean from a conch. Instead...

You cunt...

fist against flesh, a dull thud like a large heart

and I'm cocooned, encased by the hundreds of stories that are ~~unraveling~~ accumulating all around me. I can feel them against the walls, can sense them the way one can sense February storms, when you know the drifts of snow are trellising up the walls of the house, keeping you confined. I ~~fight~~ resist the urge to walk next door, simply knock on the door and say, *Can I*

help what though? We'd all end up stuck in those hexagon-shaped combs again anyway (it is a hexagon, right? Not an octagon? I'm trying to remember how it all fits).

but writing you this (even from so far away) makes me feel less alone. And I have an embarrassing confession — on the nights when I can't fall asleep, I spray some of your cologne (I ~~stole~~ took your travel-sized bottle with me) on the inside of my wrist and keep it curled close to my face. It's my comfort and it helps

~~please~~ but don't think less of me

Letter from Baucis

Archivist's Note:
MsC 073-03. Written on light blue stationery with pencil. Handwriting is blurry and suggests either a hurried hand or writing done in darkness.

But how was I to know that you would refuse to occupy the space I carved out for you in my life?

In your absence I only remember the good moments (perhaps these were the only memories I felt I could carry with me this far) — how you explained to me all the variances of my iris, every nuance, every fleck. How I kept my eyes closed so I could record your voice, spooling it in behind my ear, deep in memory. And you ~~scared~~ terrified me. I think when someone really sees you *(really sees you)* it is always frightening.

that small clay horse on the ~~shelf~~ ~~counter~~ dresser that my cousin sent me before she died, the books on the left side of the third hallway shelf (from Neruda over), my set of silver grapefruit spoons

I'll pick it up upon my return or will send someone to grab the box.

Thank you.

Letter from Chloe

Archivist's Note: MsC 073-04. Written on scrap of cardstock with severely dog-eared corners with red ballpoint pen. Handwriting loose and casual.

A man stood near to me in the museum as I tried to drown myself in water lilies (Do you remember that afternoon? The pond? The music?). Too near, his warmth spreading over my shoulders, his breath heaving in my ear. He smelled musty, of black licorice and wet mohair. Traces of cigarette smoke. ~~It made me nostalgic for you.~~ It made me uncomfortable and, even though I wanted to, I walked away without looking back at him. There are some things you shouldn't take, some things you don't want to fold away and carry with you. You only have so many pockets, so many spaces to store things.

~~remember?~~ Did I ever tell you that I believe every person we ever see falls to rest somewhere inside us, like coins drifting down in a fountain? I am overflowing with crowds, with patterns of faces and yet there are so few I retrieve, so few I finger, so few I even choose to remember.

Letter from Diomira

Archivist's Note: MsC 073-05. Written on what appears to be a back page torn from a book with green ink and perfect script. Severe water damage at the edges of the page caused ink to bleed profusely, especially towards the bottom of the letter.

and everything smelled like decaying books and my legs ached like they did in childhood. That memory of growth

I bought a book but it was raining. I had to find a way to hide it beneath my clothes, find a way to shelter it with my body

I remember you in strange ways like that last night in September when I embraced you to say goodbye, my face pressed against your neck and I remember how the spot just behind your earlobe smelled of wet leaves.

I think I'm remembering how to love you, however imperfectly

and it was at that moment that I realized *I am happy.* And as soon as I thought, *This is happiness* it had already begun to evapora

Letter from Isidora

Archivist's Note:
MsC 073-07. Written on thin lined transparent paper with black ink. Spidery handwriting hurried and uneven. Due to condition, manuscript too delicate to handle by hand.

I once imagined making love to a woman I barely knew. Imagined the framed blueprints of our bodies misfitting, soft parts against mirrored softness, angle of hip bones grinding together. But I think the kisses would have been gentler, perhaps more glancing.

but I prefer the way you held me, all your hard planes against all my soft parts. A different kind of misfit.

I thought it was ~~beautiful~~ intriguing.

I want

and perhaps then I could find a happiness that would fit the ribs.

when all I want is to find the angles, to understand the geometry of relationship.

Letter from Raissa

Archivist's Note:
MsC 073-08. Written on unidentifiable vellum with gray ink that is only readable when held up to a light. Manuscript should only be viewed under specialized lamps (see supplementary endnotes for further instruction).

I wonder about the catalogue of confluences that has led me here, ~~that tether us together~~. All those tenuous nets. No matter how much we want it, we can never be untangled now.

the way parallel blood vessels form to accommodate a damaged heart

etched in the back of the door "I adore thee" and two hand spans below "jamais" and I wonder what happened in the unwritten space between

I couldn't resist entering the store that claimed to sell possibilities. When I asked the woman tending the counter, she pulled two dusty bundles of unopened letters all dated from eons ago from a shelf and placed them in front of me. I asked her how buying an unopened letter was purchasing possibility and she replied, "Keep the letter sealed and you will ~~imagine~~ wonder at the stories it may contain. All those possibilities." I bought three — one for me and one

characters in books lead lives we crave but are afraid of.

I think I remember reading a story by Kawabata about "a mirror in the bottom of a bathtub" – such a strange image and yet I cannot ~~purge~~ forget

Letter from Thekla

Archivist's Note:
MsC 073-09. Written on handmade paper with charcoal pencil that has caused handwriting to become severely smudged. Manuscript must be handled with gloves. Hold only at the edges.

A large moth flew into my window tonight, its wings a powdered copper. It reminded me of the months after my father died and our house became infested with moths, dusted gray wings fluttering as soon as shadows fell through the rooms. My mother chased them furiously, as if they represented another kind of illness, one she had a chance to heal. But in the end she failed; they ate through the Persian rugs with a calculated slowness, the colorful patterns deteriorating into individual threads. It was like watching my mother's world disintegrate

I can no longer bear the smell of cedar.

when I found it dead the next morning I pressed it between the pages of my journal. I'll send it to you so

Letter from Zaira

Archivist's Note:
MsC 073-10. Written on blank back of torn out magazine ad of a woman wrapped in a piece of beige cloth, origin unknown. Only letter with printed writing. Blue ink used.

Sadly, I knew I was ravenous for any kind of contact when the young woman who sells Siamese Fighting Fish in plastic cups on the corner ran her finger over the lines of my palm as though these were sentences apprehensible through touch (I wanted more than a future from her) and noted that I would finally

had some concoction of noodles and spiced vegetables — so hot my mouth felt as if all the skin had been seared from its interior. The walls were covered in vintage horror movie posters: giant death bats, vampires with their seductive stealth, zombies jolting forward awkwardly. All their corners were torn, peeling. But it was the poster of Frankenstein that struck me because he looked more sad than frightening — the overhang of brow bone shadowed his eyes and made it appear that beneath the heavy stitching of cheekbone and green skin there was a man trapped within the hideous carapace, evident only in those despondent hazel eyes staring out from the monster's visage

my waiter wore a shirt that had *This is me now* written across its front. He placed a fortune cookie on my bill. I almost didn't want to open it, had had too much future for one day. But I did. It read, *Today everything changes*. Today. I am still waiting.

at the edge of the fountain I noticed a tattoo on a man's foot that ran up his ankle written in script (Old English font, I believe): *Without Love We Perish*. I thought him ~~frightening~~ off-putting until I read this – then I just found him

Can you believe there is a street here named *Ekphrasis*?

Letter from Zobeide

Archivist's Note:
MsC 073-11. Written on length of high bond paper, top and bottom tearing suggests page torn to size. Handwriting is open and looping, lines not particularly straight. Maroon coloured ink used. Because of length, manuscript must be laid out on a long, flat surface to be read. Water damage to signature extensive. A ghost of a letter under microscope suggests either a W or V.

opened the drawer and instead of a bible, I found *The Dictionary of Miracles*: stories of

tears flowing backwards, hands

limbs knit back together

forgotten for hundreds of years until

feathers torn from angel

fish, resurrected

there is a legend about how this city was built, only no one remembers it. Nonetheless every long-term resident claims there is a legend, even though not a single person has been able to recount it. They only know it exists, like that one memory, film thin, you can sense in your mind, tenuously stored in the labyrinth of your neurons and to find it you must know the twisting route that will lead you back, the passwords and keys, and finally how to hold it up to the light. The closest I came was an old man in the market (his face was fantastic, like a crumpled newspaper, you know – worn and lived) who told me that

Isn't that amazing? As with all legends, I believe there is some truth to this myth.

I don't know ~~how~~ if I shall find my way home again

~~With Love~~ ~~Yours~~ Be Well,

Notes on Poems

Translations of *Schlucke Deine Stiche:*

15.02.68

I have moved to the terrace
with my typewriter
in an attempt to write you a letter,
I say attempt
because I am unsure if I will finish this today —
I want to tell you so much,
to write about my thoughts,
since I am hardly physically occupied
I have so much more time
to move through my thoughts
and I want to be able to share these all with you.

20.03.68

Yesterday was my 29th birthday —
not exactly an earth-shattering experience.

That means I have become old —
actually older, although I don't feel I've aged much
just ripened.

Even the resume that I could write now
wouldn't exactly be overwhelming
as my achievements thus far have been thin at best.

The time has come to begin something.

Easier said than done.

22.03.68

You'll notice
how often I write
about these kinds of artistic achievements —
I would like to bring something into being
with my writing.
Often, when I dream in the sun,
or when I am about to fall asleep,
I have ideas that I can clearly
transform into sentences
including the punctuation —
it is as if I were already writing
and that these lines were worth
being printed and carried into the future
although this may sound
arrogant coming from my lips.

03.04.68

Often I want to attempt
to bring these thoughts to paper
but as soon as I really think about these things
even the choice between typewriter
or handwriting
is problematic
and it seems as if these thoughts
filter out of my mind
and away
as if through a sieve.
I don't know
if they are of the opinion
that they are not worthy
of being brought to paper.

15.04.68

Perhaps I have expressed myself somewhat pompously here
but that may have to do with the fact
that the writer, if one even sleeps within me,
has not yet awoken
although the sentences are as clear for me
as the eyes of our children.

Maybe these lines will also be clear for you
which would then give me hope,
for at least one person,
who has an advantage over all others
as she is there, tuned in to the same wavelength as me,
that for her I could write clearly.

04.05.68

Often I catch myself
writing poems about you, for you,
something that may never reach the page
but that shows me
all the things that exist within me
that I would never have discovered otherwise.
Is that a sign of insanity
                                        or eccentricity?
          I'm not sure.

25.05.68

It is wonderfully isolated there —
only large black crabs and the spray
of the surf. My writing becomes a force
because only then am I in the mood to write.
Then the words come, the thoughts come,
and I write many versions
on various topics.

When I return to the village, I tear up everything I've written
because I no longer believe in it.
Are these feelings of inferiority?
Or am literarily
                    barren?
I am not sure but I will continue my attempts
to bring something worthwhile to bear.

26.06.68

My book
has not
progressed further —
currently
there's nothing in it.

But I don't want to abandon
the hope
that one day
this knot will break.

02.07.68

Tell me what you think,
you don't need to spare me
because nothing is more dangerous
than living alone in those castles in the air.

One must eventually
        return to earth —

no matter how beautiful the former may be.

07.07.68

I feel every line you write,

swallow your pain.

Sectional Epigraphs:

Ackerman, Diane. Taken from: *An Alchemy of Mind: The Marvel and Mystery of the Brain.* New York: Scribner, 2004.

Amichai, Yehuda. Taken from: "You Too Got Tired." *The Selected Poetry of Yehuda Amichai.* New York: HarperCollins, 1986.

Calvino, Italo. Taken from: *Invisible Cities.* London: Vintage, 1997.

Crozier, Lorna. Taken from: "A Word About the Poem." (1995-2006). *Random House.* Retrieved October 13, 2006, from http://www.randomhouse.com/catlogdisplay.pperl?isbn9780771024672&view=excerpt

Manguel, Alberto. Taken from: *A Reading Diary.* Toronto: Knopf, 2004.

Ondaatje, Michael. *Divisadero.* Toronto: McClelland & Stewart, 2007.

Shorris, Earl. Taken from: "The Last Word: Can the World's Small Languages Be Saved?" *Harper's Magazine.* Vol. 301, No. 1803: August, 2000 (43).

Poem Epigraphs:

Connelly, Karen. Taken from: "This Dumb Melodrama." *The Disorder of Love.* Toronto: Gutter Press, 1997.

Howes, David. Taken from: Introduction to *Empire of the Senses: The Sensual Culture Reader.* Oxford: Berg, 2005.

Shorris, Earl. Taken from: "The Last Word: Can the World's Small Languages Be Saved?" *Harper's Magazine.* Vol. 301, No. 1803: August, 2000 (43).

About the Author

Vanessa Moeller's poems and short stories have appeared in numerous periodicals including *The Fiddlehead, Prism International, The Antigonish Review, CV2, The Pottersfield Portfolio* and *Qwerty* and have won several awards including the W.F.N.S's 2002 Atlantic Poetry Prize. She completed her MA in creative writing at the University of New Brunswick. She now lives in Fredericton, New Brunswick.